W(h)ine

50 PERFECT WINES TO PAIR WITH
YOUR CHILD'S ROTTEN BEHAVIOR

Jennifer Todryk
CREATOR OF *LIFE AS A RAMBLING REDHEAD*

W(h)ine

50 PERFECT WINES TO PAIR WITH
YOUR CHILD'S ROTTEN BEHAVIOR

Jennifer Todryk

CREATOR OF *LIFE AS A RAMBLING REDHEAD*

Race Point
PUBLISHING

Brimming with creative inspiration, how-to projects, and useful information to enrich your everyday life, Quarto Knows is a favorite destination for those pursuing their interests and passions. Visit our site and dig deeper with our books into your area of interest: Quarto Creates, Quarto Cooks, Quarto Homes, Quarto Lives, Quarto Drives, Quarto Explores, Quarto Gifts, or Quarto Kids.

Text © 2017 by Jennifer Todryk
Illustrations © 2017 by Eda Kaban

First published in 2017 by Race Point Publishing,
an imprint of The Quarto Group
142 West 36th Street, 4th Floor
New York, NY 10018 USA
www.QuartoKnows.com

ISBN 978-1-63106-335-0

Editorial Director: Jeannine Dillon
Project Editor: Jason Chappell
Art Director: Merideth Harte
Design: 3&Co.

10 9 8 7 6 5 4 3

Printed in China

CONTENTS

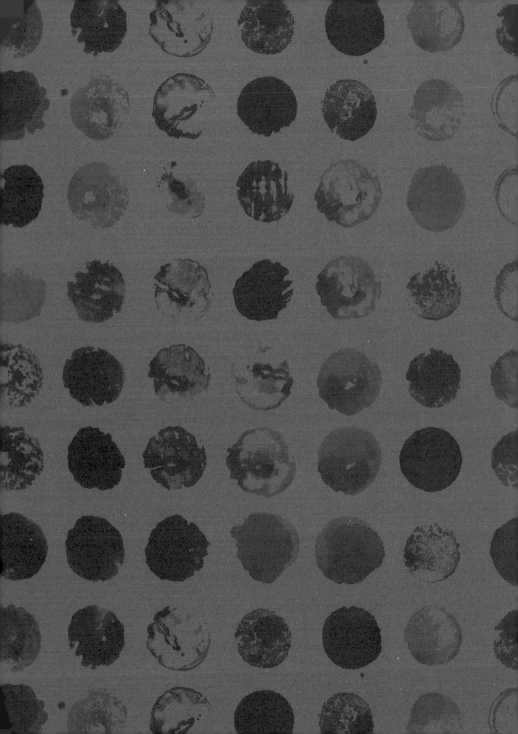

If I could ask a favor from all the lovely people out there . . .
I need you to wear the best sarcasm-lovin' pants that you own
and not take what you are about to read as sound medical
advice. I love wine, and I have a feeling that you're fond of it
too, since you've got a copy of this spectacular book in your
hands. But by no means am I promoting alcoholism or actually
suggesting that drinking wine in large quantities or in an
unsafe manner will make parenting any easier (too bad,
right?). I am, however, a big believer in wine humor and
calling my children baby-beasts, so let's just have some fun
here and try to make some unpleasant parenting situations
 a little funnier.
       Because who doesn't think explosive newborn
poop is funny?

Cheers!

Jennifer Todryk

INTRODUCTION

Whether you were gifted this book by a vino-loving friend or bought it out of sheer parenting desperation, I am hopeful and almost positive that this book will make your life better. It looks fantastic in your hands, after all. Almost as good as a wine glass! (well, almost.)

After all, if you're a wine mom or wine dad, then you know that there is almost nothing better than a glass of wine at the end of a crappy day. And that's exactly why I wrote this book. Pairing your child's crappy behavior with wine doesn't stop the crappy from happening. But if remembering that there is always a wine to pair with your child's grocery store meltdown or that there are other wine parents out there trying to power through some appallingly bad behavior from their kids (yup, been there, done that!), then my job is done here. Most of the pairings in this book are for parents, but because there are so many teachers out there who also deal with kids all day, I have included two special bonus pairings just for teachers (see pages 75 and 87).

Before we go any further, I should say at the outset that this is a *humor* book. I am not encouraging parents to drink all the time nor am I advising you to drink in an unsafe manner. And while this book is, of course, about the world's most heavenly beverage, it is also about laughter and solidarity. We love our kids to death. Of course we do! But they can also be a royal pain in the ass. Being able to laugh at how ridiculous kids can be sometimes can help take you out of a furious moment. So if this book makes you laugh or helps you start the morning with an attitude of "Hello, day. Bring it on!" then I will be one happy wine mom.

And speaking of wine moms, how do you know if you qualify as one? Wine parents have can-do attitudes. They conquer each day like a parenting warrior, passing out lunches, timeouts, the occasional eye roll, and kisses like it's their *job* (because, um, I guess it *is*.) And let's be honest, if you magically stumbled on this book, that's a pretty good indication that you're exhibiting some tannin tendencies.

Or maybe you're a wine mom and didn't even know it until now. Maybe you're reading these words of wisdom while enjoying a glass of Pinot with a sleeve of Pringles (*I mean, I think you know where you stand, ladies*). And just so we're clear, being a wine mom doesn't mean you must drink wine daily or that you consume wine 24/7. I'm a mother of two toddlers who maybe has time to enjoy one or two glasses a week. But when I do drink, you better believe it's wine. That's because I'm a wine mom. If you're not sure if you qualify, take the quiz on the next page and see where you stand.

—Jennifer Todryk
CREATOR OF *LIFE AS A RAMBLING REDHEAD*

TOP 21 SIGNS YOU'RE
A WINE MOM (OR DAD)!

Take a look at the quiz below and check off the boxes that you can relate to. (Seriously, check the boxes. This is a legit personality test given to us by experts and many, many important people who we can't name.)

○ 1. You like wine. Obviously.

○ 2. You're a mom. Or a dad. (If you checked off this box and the box above, there is an 85 percent chance you're already wine mom or dad, according to our very real, not at all imagined, experts.)

○ 3. When given the choice of consuming an alcoholic beverage, most— if not all—of the time you choose wine.

○ 4. When at a Mexican restaurant, you always choose sangria because you like to respect the drinking choices of other countries and cultures (but only if they involve wine).

○ 5. You know that some states have pharmacies that sell wine. So basically, it's acceptable for you to consider it medicine.

○ 6. You classify your entire day based on its wine potential: "It's a wine kind of night" or "I've earned some wine today."

○ 7. When you say, "These children drive me to drink," you are speaking quite literally and you are, of course, referring only to wine.

○ 8. You collect corks and consider them visually pleasing home décor.

○ 9. You keep empty wine bottles and turn them into pretty things . . . which are really just wine bottles covered in paint and burlap.

○ 10. You think wine is the classiest of alcoholic beverages. Yes, even when it comes in a box.

O 11. You keep suggesting Napa Valley as a vacation spot for your family even though there aren't chicken nuggets or children's rides within 30 miles of this heaven on earth.

O 12. You have thought about putting wine in a travel coffee mug or sippy cup and drinking while at the park.

O 13. You have put wine in a travel coffee mug or sippy cup and drank it while at the park.

O 14. Your friends text or message you funny wine memes they find online because it "made them think of you."

O 15. You have contemplated whether an aerator makes a suitable gift for your child's teacher.

O 16. You understand that wine calories don't count.

O 17. All right, fine, you acknowledge wine has calories, but you just don't give a damn.

O 18. You are a member of a wine club. Or two.

O 19. You are not a member of a wine club because you tried that once, and they only sent you 2 or 3 bottles a month (wtf?).

O 20. You see wine as an acceptable beverage of choice because, after all, most religions embrace it for one reason or another (yes, God approves).

O 21. White or red? The answer is YES.

So how did you do? If you can relate to any of the things on this very official wine personality test, then it's safe to say that you're down with the vino-life. And that means you should keep reading for the best parenting advice you're ever going to get. You can thank me later, friend. Or better yet, just raise a glass to me in your next toast (tonight).

SCREW IT!

HOW TO OPEN A WINE BOTTLE
WITHOUT A CORKSCREW

I'm sure you've been there. You just purchased a bottle of delicious wine, settled in on the couch with your husband and some binge-worthy Netflix only to discover that you can't find a freaking corkscrew. I cannot convey the anger, desperation, and utter frustration of these darkest of moments. But thanks to desperate people worldwide (and Google), there is a light at the end of the cork. These are my four favorite methods for busting into a wine bottle, sans corkscrew. The first time you try these tactics you may not be very polished, but with some practice (and dedication to consuming wine), anyone can become a cork-removal master.

Who knows, you may never want to use a corkscrew again, because the blowtorch is way more fun.

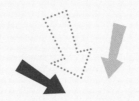

The Shoe-Fly Method

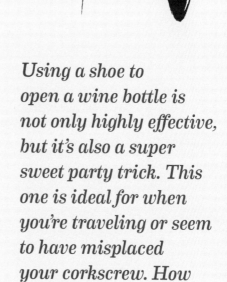

SUPPLIES NEEDED

- A wine bottle with a cork
- A shoe (men's shoe or tennis shoe with padding)
- A sturdy wall
- A functioning human arm

Using a shoe to open a wine bottle is not only highly effective, but it's also a super sweet party trick. This one is ideal for when you're traveling or seem to have misplaced your corkscrew. How could you?!

STEP 1:

Take the wine bottle and place the bottom end in the heel of a shoe.

STEP 2:

Holding the wine bottle in place in the shoe, beat the sole of the shoe against the sturdy wall. The shoe serves as a barrier between wine bottle and the wall. Since you are a classy and intelligent wine drinker, you know that pounding a wine bottle against a wall without the shoe as protection would end up a very sad, stained catastrophe. We want to drink the wine, not decorate with it.

STEP 3:

Continue beating the shoe (with the wine bottle inside it) against the wall and observe as the cork slowly rises.

STEP 4:

When the cork has risen enough for you to grasp it, pull it out of the bottle. Warning: The wine may splatter when you pull out the cork.

STEP 5:

Drink the wine and be proud of what you've done. This is the most satisfying step of all!

The Flashdance Method

SUPPLIES NEEDED:

- A wine bottle with a cork
- A blowtorch
- Safety glasses
- A steady hand

This approach is perfect for all the pyromaniacs out there who happen to have a blowtorch lying around the house. No judgment.

STEP 1:

Hold your bottle of wine out in front of your body, unless you don't mind singed eyebrows, in which case hold it wherever.

STEP 2:

Light up the torch and begin applying heat to the bottle in the air-filled space between the wine and the bottom of the cork. Slowly rotate the bottle to evenly distribute heat.

STEP 3:

Observe as the cork slowly rises.

STEP 4:

When the cork has risen enough for you to grasp it, pull it out of the bottle. Warning: The wine may splatter when you pull out the cork.

STEP 5:

Hallelujah! Pour a glass of wine for you and a loved one. Or just for you. You don't have to share if you don't want to.

The MacGyver Method

SUPPLIES NEEDED:

- A wine bottle with a cork
- A screwdriver or drill
- A large screw
- A hammer or pliers

This method is for the people who don't want to mess around. It's quick, it's easy, and it's basically the same thing as a corkscrew . . . just a tad more aggressive.

STEP 1:

Hold the wine bottle steady and use the screwdriver or drill to screw the screw into the cork. You want to put enough of the screw into the cork for it to not tear out when you pull on the screw.

STEP 2:

Use the hammer or pliers to grasp the screw and gently pull it upward. Continue to hold the bottle steady.

STEP 3:

The cork should slide right out. Oh, joy!

STEP 4:

Consume the wine and thank the screw.

The Spoon-It Method

SUPPLIES NEEDED:

- A wine bottle with a cork
- A wooden spoon (or something with the same shape)
- A paper towel
- The full strength of your body weight

This method of removing a cork is super simple, and it's the perfect solution for people who don't mind a cork floating in their wine bottle. When you don't have a corkscrew, we can't be too picky, now can we?

STEP 1:

Hold your bottle of wine out in front of your body.

STEP 2:

Take the handle of the wooden spoon and push down on the cork.

STEP 3:

Hold the wine bottle steady as you keep pushing.

STEP 4:

Watch the cork fall into your adult grape juice. Cry with glee.

STEP 5:

Cheers to our glorious wooden spoon!

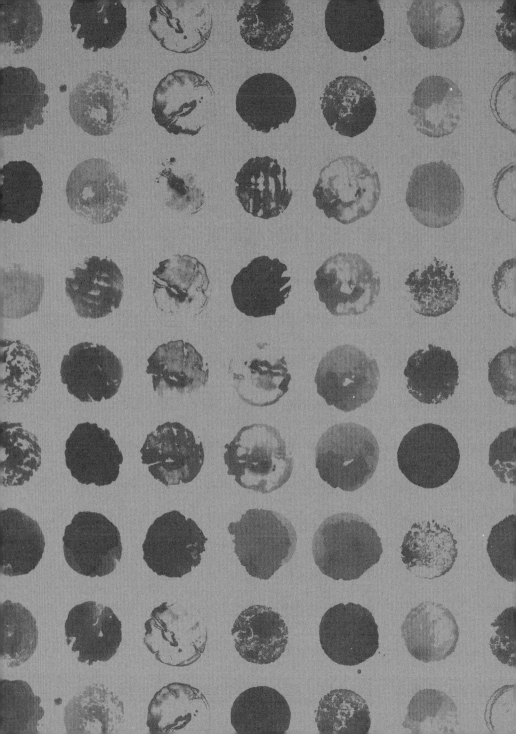

Wine Pairings

MALBEC
TEMPER TANTRUM WINE

Drink **MALBEC** *when your toddler decides to throw a hellish temper tantrum while in a very public place, like Target.*

If your toddler decided to climb on top of your car in the middle of the Target parking lot today while producing a scream that should have been recorded for a horror film, then Malbec is absolutely what should be in your glass tonight. There is nothing smooth about a public tantrum from hell, but luckily for you, Malbec has a reputation for being just that. With its soft tannins and flavors from all of the best berries, this wine is sure to make you smile. Unlike your child-beast who probably made you cry . . . at Target *(arguably one of the greatest places on Earth)*. How dare he steal your Target joy.

RIESLING
NUMBER 2 WINE

RIESLING *pairs perfectly with an explosive poopy diaper.*

If your newborn baby had an explosive bowel movement that left your hands literally shit-stained from the yellow substance we call "poop," we suggest immediately chugging a glass of Riesling. Riesling is refreshing, tends to be sweet, and has a low acidity level. You've handled enough liquid that smelled of pure acid today, so kick back and enjoy this smooth, light wine that usually possesses the smell of apples. How lovely.

CHARDONNAY
WINE WITH AN ATTITUDE

CHARDONNAY *goes great with a middle schooler's attitude adjustment.*

If your middle-school child—let's call her Megan—gave you non-stop attitude today and yelled the words, "You're the worst mom ever!" or "Why can't you be cool, like Addison's mom?!" then you would most likely benefit from a good buzz. We recommend Chardonnay for your drinking pleasure this evening. Chardonnay is described as tasting sweet, like melons, and has a subtle creaminess. Subtle creaminess sounds divine. Addison's mom sounds annoying.

PROSECCO
PARENTING ALONE WINE

Choose **PROSECCO** *when your spouse has a "mandatory" happy hour.*

When your husband's work happy hour—that he *has* to attend—happens to be on basically the worst parenting day of your life, don't waste energy texting him a paragraph of profanity. Instead throw the hooligans in bed (*extremely early*) and break out the Prosecco! This sparkling wine tastes like tart fruit juice and is no longer reserved for sipping on the patios of Italy. Wine experts are now reporting that Prosecco also pairs perfectly with any stressful weekday, like Tuesday or Wednesday. Since your children succeeded in their only life goal of sucking every ounce of energy out of your broken body, put some pep back in your step with this light and bubbly alcoholic beverage. Rip off that bra, put on your oversized sweatpants, and consume a couple glasses of Prosecco; you've just made your own damn happy hour.

MERLOT
WARRIOR WINE

Pair a MERLOT *with multiple child madness.*

If you have multiple children, and all of them decided to act like freaking lunatics on the same day, then you need something that goes down easily. Something that's easy to gulp. We suggest a Merlot. This wine is referred to as an "introducing" wine to initiate novice wine drinkers since it is smooth and light. We are very aware that you are not new to drinking wine, but tonight is not the night to jack around with a dry wine that forces you to drink slowly. You were assaulted by multiple child warriors today and you're still alive to complain about it. Drink up, soldier.

SAUVIGNON BLANC
"I SURRENDER" WINE

Choose SAUVIGNON BLANC *when your toddler uses you as target practice.*

If you were stuck inside all day with a toddler who did nothing but throw every toy in his playroom and whine about absolutely everything, then we recommend enjoying one glass (possibly two) of Sauvignon Blanc. This wine is said to have an earthy taste, such as bell peppers or freshly mowed grass. Drinking something that smells of fresh sod will surely help you forget the painful memories of toy trucks being hurled at your face or being bitten by a small baby beast who wants nothing more than to see you cry.

PINOT NOIR
AAA WINE

PINOT NOIR *goes well with dented or scratched vehicles.*

If your teenager was involved in a minor "fender-bender" today (a.k.a. she backed her new car into your car that was parked in the driveway), then we recommend a Pinot Noir. This wine is very delicate and fresh, unlike your daughter whose sole purpose in life seems to be attempting to destroy all of the cars you own. The tannins in this wine are very soft, making it the opposite of bitter. Nobody needs a dry wine when their daughter is constantly participating in a real-life game of bumper cars. . . . You're already bitter enough, thanks to her.

CABERNET SAUVIGNON
ROYALLY DISGUSTED WINE

CABERNET SAUVIGNON *pairs perfectly with poor hygiene.*

If you find yourself covered in baby vomit, human waste, or toddler boogers, then you need to drink wine that will, for a brief moment, make you feel like royalty. We suggest drinking a glass of Cabernet Sauvignon. This wine has been dubbed the king of red wines. It's dark, rich, and is said to be best when paired with a decadent, juicy steak. When one is covered in enough foul bodily fluids to alarm even the most seasoned CSI team, one has neither the time nor the desire to grill a steak. Thank goodness drinking wine does not take much effort. Forget the steak and grab your best crystal glass to have the ultimate royal experience.

✳ And don't forget to change shirts immediately. Queens and kings don't sip wines with crusty nose goop stuck to their clothing.

ZINFANDEL
HORMONE HELL WINE

Pair **ZINFANDEL** *with a hormonal preteen.*

If you spent your entire day combating dramatic meltdowns and explaining to your moody middle schooler why life just isn't fair, then we recommend throwing back a glass (or four) of Zinfandel. Studies show that the berry aroma and high tannins of this light-bodied red wine pair perfectly with the salty tears of hormonal children. This wine also has a very high alcohol content, which is an absolute must after the day you've had. Berries are delicious and heavenly. Madison's hormones are freaking dreadful.

VINHO VERDE
STICKY SITUATION WINE

VINHO VERDE *goes great with the human fecal matter that is stuck in your carpet.*

If you spent a good portion of your day trying to convince a little human to excrete into a toilet or had to pick up poop-balls off of your formerly-clean carpet, then a Vinho Verde wine will taste amazing this evening. Vinho Verde has been described as delicate and refreshing, unlike potty-training, which has been described as absolute torturous hell on earth. This Portuguese wine is said to have a slight effervescence, so we recommend consuming it all at once. Consume immediately whether warm or chilled; the professionals are certain that you won't care either way.

SYRAH
COMMON CORE WINE

Choose **SYRAH** *when homework battles have left you brain-dead and in a total state of depression.*

Whether you forced your children to complete their homework by threatening their existence or just don't know how the hell to solve that algebra equation on the stupid worksheet, we are certain that Syrah will put you at ease. With its high tannins and spicy kick, Syrah is said to have a delectable "punch of flavor" that is sure to bring you out of your depressive state as well as supply you with enough energy to binge-watch Netflix for a couple hours before calling it a night. Punch me, Syrah . . . before Common Core kills me.

BOXED WINE
TOO TIRED TO CARE WINE

BOXED WINE *pairs perfectly with sleep deprivation.*

If that new, precious bundle of excessive cries kept you up all night (and the night before that and the night before that), then we suggest handing the infant to your loving spouse and drinking from your favorite boxed wine before turning in this evening. The general low quality and low maintenance nature of boxed wines (we've all had Franzia Fridays) are the perfect contrast to your tiny high maintenance human who won't go down for anything. You may think that you need more sleep, but in fact you just need some wine in the fastest way possible with the least amount of trouble. Don't worry about the taste. Our extremely accurate data shows you'll be too tired to notice ... *or care.*

PINOT NOIR ROSÉ
NO SLEEP WINE

Drink **PINOT NOIR ROSÉ** *when bedtime shenanigans leave you comatose.*

When a small human has spent the majority of bedtime begging you for more water, has demanded that every book in the house be read, has nearly convinced you that she is literally starving, has had the urge to urinate four times in a twelve-minute time frame, has claimed that she can't sleep because there is not enough oxygen in her bedroom, or any other ridiculous stalling tactic she came up with in her desperate mind, we know that nothing will leave you satisfied like this delicious wine. The fruity undertones and sweet kick of this rosé perfectly compliment the tortuous games your terrorizing toddler has forced you to play. This child seriously needs to go to bed, so you can curl up too . . . with your Pinot Noir Rosé.

GAMAY
BULLSHIT WINE

GAMAY *pairs perfectly with fabricated stories.*

If your child has become quite the avid storyteller, then you should consider sipping on a glass of Gamay this evening. Whether the storytelling involves blatant lies like unfinished homework assignments and brushing his or her teeth, or something more sinister like saying, "Mommy likes to drink six glasses of wine, like, every night" to her Sunday School teacher, this wine is sure to numb the irritation. All those lies definitely leave a sour taste in your mouth, so let's counteract them with a sweet, cherry-tart note that only Gamay can deliver. If only your daughter could put her imagination to good use, like telling people you only serve your family farm-fresh organic foods. Or that you're actually twenty-nine. Until then, we recommend owning that lush title she's bestowed on you and drinking through the bullshit.

PROVENCE ROSÉ
MOMMY DEAREST WINE

Choose **PROVENCE ROSÉ** *when your child refers to you as "Mom" for the first time.*

Nothing sounds worse than your sweet baby toddler calling you "Mom" instead of "Mommy" for the first time. "Excuse me?! It's *Mommy*." Your darling child might as well have said a curse word. It's freaking dreadful. While you try to hold back those pathetic tears, reach for a bottle of Provence Rosé. (Please note that we suggest a bottle, not a glass. We know this one hurts the heart.) This pleasant, fruity wine will have you relaxed in no time and will give you all the courage you need to demand your son continue to refer to you as "Mommy" until he gets married. However, once wed, he should cut that crap out immediately because it would just make everyone uncomfortable.

MUSCAT BLANC
CINDERELLA WINE

Pair **MUSCAT BLANC** *with the constant resistance to doing household chores.*

When your darling offspring—let's call him Tyler—"forgets" about his chores on the family to-do list despite multiple reminders, then a full-size glass of Muscat Blanc needs to be in your immediate future. Nothing leaves a bitter taste in your mouth and an unpleasant scowl on your face like a child who refuses any kind of responsibility. Tonight, chase down all the bitterness with a wine that has been described as tasting like sweet tropical honey. This delicate drink has flat acidity, which is perfect since your anti-chore hellion puts enough spice in your life. Hand the kid a mop and then hand yourself a wine glass because the only thing on your to-do list this evening is Muscat.

PINOT GRIGIO
THE NOOOOOOOOOOO WINE

Pair a **PINOT GRIGIO** *with excessive use of the word "No."*

If you have "NO" embedded in your brain due to your family's overuse of the word, then Pinot Grigio needs to be your wine of choice this evening and possibly the rest of the year. Pinot Grigio's primary fruit flavors tend to be pear, apple, and melon, which are said to taste joyful on the tongue. The word "NO" that you and your small baby beasts throw at each other all day long tastes like irritating, repetitive poison when on your tongue. Sipping blissfully on a glass of Pinot will definitely help drown out this obnoxious word, at least until the next morning. Pinot Grigio? NO YES.

CÔTES DU RHÔNE
NO NAP WINE

CÔTES DU RHÔNE *pairs perfectly with a strong refusal to take a nap.*

A toddler protesting a nap may be one of the strongest acts of disobedience that can drive parents across the globe to drink. Despite the fact that he is barely functioning, running into furniture, and crying hysterically because you broke his cracker in half (instead of giving it to him whole, of course), your toddler is still refusing to lie down and take a freaking nap. In order to drown out this horrible devil-like behavior, experts recommend Côtes du Rhône, a soft red wine that exudes a tobacco smell and has a smoky aftertaste. Sure, you quit smoking sometime between school and this fresh hell, but nap time troubles require a serious wine. And if that serious wine smells like the smoky tobacco of your yesteryear, then drink up, my friend.

ROSADO "MY" WINE

Pair ROSADO *with your child's inability to share.*

When your child seems physically unable to share anything in his possession—whether it's his favorite toy or just something he stole from his sister because she seemed to be enjoying it too much—we suggest enjoying a glass of Rosado to wash away any tension that the child has left behind. Data shows that excessive use of the word "MINE," especially when screamed by a manic toddler, can definitely cause innocent mothers a great deal of stress. Rosado is bright and sweet, making this Spanish Rosé extremely easy to enjoy . . . unlike your rude toddler, who is turning a fun play date into a freaking nightmare. Share the toys, but let's not share the Rosado . . . "That's mine."

LAGREIN
THE DMV WINE

Choose **LAGREIN** *when your child is armed with a new driver's license.*

If riding in the passenger seat of your car with your sixteen-year-old daughter behind the wheel made you realize that she just might be a threat to humanity, then Lagrein needs to be your drink of choice this evening. Just the fact that she almost took out a stop sign, a neighbor's dog, and Mr. Williams— all within a seventeen-minute driving lesson—instantly awards you a glass of this spicy red wine. Lagrein has been described as tasting like black pepper and gravel, which will pair perfectly with today's horrifying joyride. Twist off that screw top, pour yourself a glass, and deliver the news to your daughter that you see a bus in her future.

BANDOL
POP STAR WINE

Drink **BANDOL** *when your child's dream of becoming the next YouTube sensation is just too much.*

If your preteen daughter believes that she is the next Selena Gomez and questions why the family won't move to Los Angeles to support her promising career as a YouTube star, then Bandol is what should be in your wine glass tonight. All she wants to do is sing, take selfies, and instantly get famous, and how dare you get in the way of her God-given talent. Statistics show that this dark, rich, peppery wine compliments dream-crushing immaculately, making it the perfect beverage to drink after trying to explain to your young superstar that you have this commitment called a job. Little does she know, you need this job in order to feed her adorable starlet face. For now she will have to continue practicing her singing in the shower while you sit back with your Bandol and request that everyone in the house refer to you as Queen Dream Killer.

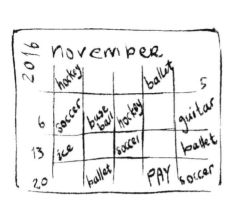

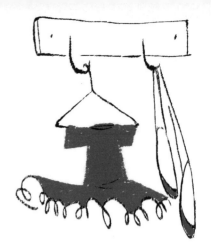

GRENACHE BLANC
BROKE WINE

GRENACHE BLANC *pairs perfectly with the ridiculous cost of your child's extracurricular activities.*

When the monthly cost of all of your child's extracurricular activities becomes more expensive than your house payment, experts strongly recommend stocking up on bottles of Grenache Blanc. This light, lemony wine will sweeten just about any financial predicament, which is absolutely necessary for you since your child wants to join every team or group that is offered at school. Unless your child is a fundraising beast and sells 72,852 coupon books, 953 boxes of candy bars, and 3,629 rolls of holiday wrapping paper, your house may go into foreclosure. With Grenache Blanc in hand, it's time to break the news to your overactive teen that he must choose only two activities because unfortunately not everyone is a millionaire. Life just sucks that way.

SHERRY
KILL ME NOW WINE

Choose **SHERRY** *when you feel less than dignified in your large-and-in-charge minivan.*

If you're feeling a little insecure about trading in the last remains of your self-respect for the large minivan that is now parked in your driveway, sherry is what needs to be on the dinner menu this evening. This dessert wine will have you feeling fancy in no time with its strong flavor and slightly higher alcohol content. Statistics show that if you drink enough sherry in one sitting, you will actually start to believe that you are royalty, even in your goldish-brown minivan. After all, only royalty like yourself would drive a vehicle with sixteen cup holders, slick no-touch sliding doors, enough space to transport the entire neighborhood (because that sounds swell), and pull-down shades that are sure to satisfy any bored toddler for hours. Who needs a sexy sports car when you have your super sweet momvan . . . err, minivan. Your spacious oval chariot awaits you, Your Highness.

PINOTAGE
PICKY EATER WINE

Drink **PINOTAGE** *when dinnertime battles leave you in an intense state of frustration.*

When your toddler refuses to eat what you spent the last two hours of your life cooking for dinner, and only seems interested in foods that are in the form of a nugget or a pizza, we suggest partaking in a glass of Pinotage. This spicy red wine has been described as tasting like blueberries and blackberries, which experts now say compliment the denial of vegetables perfectly. How dare you physically assault a toddler's mouth with anything green and unfried? Forget that sixteen-step Food Network chicken and broccoli recipe, assemble that peanut butter and jelly sandwich you make so flawlessly, and embrace a liquid dinner for yourself. Tonight, there shall be no green on the menu, only dark red.

WHITE ZINFANDEL
SELECTIVE HEARING WINE

Choose **WHITE ZINFANDEL** *when your husband seems unable to hear the screaming baby in the monitor.*

When your husband seems to have mysteriously lost his hearing from eleven at night to seven in the morning, experts suggest throwing back a glass of White Zinfandel whenever the hell you feel like it. Scientists aren't sure why husbands are able to sleep through the constant cries of a newborn in the middle of the night, but they do know that this sweet rosé goes down easy, just like your spouse. Tonight, after you throw back your White Zinfandel, maybe throw a kick to your husband's ass when that baby monitor starts sounding. The baby might not be able to wake him from slumber, but your foot sure can.

FREISA
WINE THAT BITES BACK

FREISA *pairs perfectly with teething terrors.*

If your normally happy infant is experiencing teething troubles, then we recommend consuming a few glasses of Freisa to help heal the heartache. It's horrible to watch your infant be so miserable and it's even worse to be up at all hours of the night with a screaming child who you can do nothing to console. They need those teeth, like you need this wine. With its fresh taste and strong tannins, this red wine will have you more patient in no time. We recommend you keep a few of these bottles on hand since teeth tend to pop up out of nowhere. And you'll need to pop that cork out just as fast.

CABERNET FRANC
EINSTEIN WINE

Choose CABERNET FRANC *when you have a know-it-all teenager.*

Life can be almost unbearable when you live with a teenager who believes that he's is more intelligent than you are. Good news! Studies now show that parents who drink a glass of Cabernet Franc when they have a real know-it-all monster can deal with the constant bullshit for longer periods of time. This wine is both medium-bodied and well-balanced, making it very easy to drink (but you wouldn't know this because you're too stupid, of course). This preferred drink of dummies like yourself is best served at room temperature and tastes most flavorful when consumed in the presence of obnoxious teenagers. Bottoms up, dummy.

SYRAH ROSÉ
GET ME OUTTA HERE WINE

SYRAH ROSÉ *goes great with a traveling spouse.*

I f you have a spouse whose job requires a good amount of traveling, then we suggest treating yourself to some Syrah Rosé this evening. This savory dry wine has been proven to pair perfectly with strong resentment and jealous thoughts. In fact, data shows that women who drink this wine in their husband's absence tend to be more relaxed and less likely to kill him. We know that you would love to travel the world and sleep soundly in four-star hotels (hell, you would sleep in a Super 8 Motel if it meant seven hours of uninterrupted sleep) but you can't due to the humans you birthed. Apparently, they need to be watched basically every minute of the day. So stay in tonight, because you have no choice, and drink a couple of glasses of Syrah Rosé. Let's mentally travel to a happier place. No spouses allowed.

VERDEJO
DUCK LIPS WINE

Choose VERDEJO *when your kid is obsessed with getting a cellphone.*

I f your child's only purpose in life seems to be acquiring a cellphone, then we recommend partaking in a glass or two of Verdejo this evening. Verdejo is a white wine with sharp acidity and a fresh lemony aftertaste that pairs perfectly with begging and ugly-face crying. While taking endless selfies and sending emoji-only texts to friends seems extremely important to your daughter and her social status, getting your obsessed child to bed and your hands on a bottle of Verdejo is very important to you. Instead of adding yet another phone line to your quickly growing family plan, why not add another glass of wine to your life? Verdejo is the much cheaper, tastier option. Your bank account will thank you.

CHENIN BLANC
TEACHER WINE

Choose **CHENIN BLANC** *when the children in your classroom never seem to know what the hell they are doing.*

I f you find yourself standing in front of twenty-two miniature humans who repeatedly ask you, "What are we doing?" throughout the day, experts are certain that Chenin Blanc will restore most of your sanity. You just gave a lesson that is worthy of a damn Oscar award, and now Ryan is asking you what he is supposed to be doing . . . as if that wasn't what you'd just spent the past fifteen minutes explaining. This floral, fruity wine has medium acidity making it the perfect pairing for sour things, like the children who sit in your classroom and haven't got a clue. Time to start the countdown to June and drink up, teach. A for effort, right?

BARBERA
LITTLE LEAGUE WINE

Pair **BARBERA** *with your child's super exciting sporting events.*

When you find yourself at one of your child's little league games, surrounded by loudmouthed parents who seem to believe that they are unofficial "bleacher coaches," we know that Barbera will taste lovely to you this evening. This acidic red wine exudes a fresh, crisp taste and is said to pair beautifully with waking up at the ass-crack of dawn and being outside in uncomfortably cold temperatures. After a long day of toting around multiple bags of sporting equipment, watching your son pick flowers out in left field, and enduring painfully slow doubleheader games with final scores of 0–1, it's time to kick back with a refreshing glass of Barbera. Guaranteed to be the most exciting part of your extremely long day.

✳ By the way, experts say that this wine tastes fantastic when sipped in secret out of a travel coffee cup. Barbera for the win!

VIOGNIER
WASHABLE WINE

VIOGNIER *pairs beautifully with toddler vandalism.*

If your adorable tot tried to channel their inner Picasso with a permanent marker on your sofa, then Viognier may be able to reduce some of your angst. After all, seeing graffiti on your brand new Pottery Barn living room furniture could drive anyone to drink. The citrus aroma of this soft wine will temporarily remove you from your infuriated state and it tastes excellent at any time of day. Let's burn all the markers and drink all the Viognier. One day you'll be able to have nice things . . . just not today.

CAVA
BEND OVER WINE

Choose **CAVA** *when your child is potty-trained.*

So, your child is finally doing their business on a toilet like a human should ... CONGRATS! Experts have revealed that Cava sparkling wine is the perfect bubbly accessory for your potty-training celebrations. You can drink this balanced wine alone or add it to your favorite fruit juice to create a spritzy cocktail. So ditch the diapers and try to not think about how much money Pampers made off of your child's ass (literally) over the past few years. Say farewell to the stinky diaper pails and start practicing the phrase, "Bend over and let me wipe your butt," because that's your future. You thought diapers were brutal? On to poop-filled Mickey Mouse underpants. Cheers!

WHITE MERLOT
BIRDS & BEES WINE

WHITE MERLOT *pairs perfectly with uncomfortable sex talks.*

If staring your adolescent child in the eyes while talking about vaginal canals and penises was a part of your day, then we suggest White Merlot for your escape drink of choice tonight. This light bodied wine is said to be energizing to those who have recently experienced extreme perspiration, and it tastes amazing after the excessive use of words beginning with the letter "V." You've admired your child's curiosity her entire life up until this moment, but all these questions have left you feeling violated. Take a break from your condom-covered banana and subpar, made-up-on-the-spot sex analogies and reach for a bottle of White Merlot instead. Because let's be honest, you're never going to eat another banana again.

BOURGOGNE
UNDERWIRE WINE

Choose **BOURGOGNE** *when you think your nipples may fall off.*

It comes as no surprise to us that breast-feeding mothers tend to be in constant pain, and whether it's from a newborn's killer latch or a baby's killer teeth it's never welcome. Bourgogne (sometimes called "Burgundy") is a soft red wine that has been described as having chewy tannins, deep flavor, and compliments bloody and chapped nipples beautifully. Statistics show that nine out of ten women found that drinking a glass of Bourgogne after their child stops breast-feeding can take off the edge without removing their nipples. Tonight, get in on the suckling action and suck down a good size glass of Bourgogne like your abused boobs depend on it. *Because they do.*

FIANO
"F" IS FOR "FECES" WINE

Pair **FIANO** *with nap time poop-painting.*

If you walked into your child's bedroom after nap time today and witnessed poop in places that poop should never be, then Fiano needs to be in your wine glass tonight. Studies show that this dry white wine possesses a floral perfume and compliments both rancid odors and surfaces coated in human shit. Experts say that wiping excreted corn and peas off a child's crib can be a traumatic experience for both mom and vegetarian alike, and we believe that Fiano can help ward off any early onset symptoms of PTSD. We recommend drinking a glass a night to help keep the horrific images from resurfacing, while also avoiding vegetables for at least a month. Fiano is your best chance for a healthy recovery.

ROUSSANNE
STALKER WINE

ROUSSANNE *pairs well with the inability to obtain personal space.*

If your kids (or students!) seem unable to understand the concept of personal space, even though you've explained it eighteen times in the past two hours, then we recommend picking up some Roussanne on your way home tonight. This white wine is said to embody an herbal tea note that tends to turn slightly nutty over time, just like you will if Thomas taps your shoulder one more damn time. Roussanne is perfect if your toes are constantly stepped on, your desk is surrounded at all times, you're stalked during recess, followed in the halls, knocked on as if you're a front door, and basically any other form of personal space abuse. After being touched by dozens of children who keep accidentally calling you "Mom," the only thing that should be touching you tonight is a bottle of Roussanne.

UGNI BLANC
NO TALENT WINE

Choose **UGNI BLANC** *when your child starts "playing" a new instrument.*

If the repetitive blows from your son's new trumpet have you praying for sudden onset hearing loss, experts are positive that Ugni Blanc can keep you thinking clearly. Unlike your son's musical runs, this white wine is remarkably smooth and non-threatening to your cochleas. Ugni Blanc can make any off-key note seem just a bit more enjoyable because of its fruity aroma and citrusy punch. So grab a bottle of Ugni Blanc and pop the cork. That's a sound that is nothing less than fantastic.

BAROLO
CHANGE THE LOCKS WINE

Choose **BAROLO** *when your kid just can't seem to stay away.*

If your child seems unable to move out and stay out, then Barolo is the wine for you. Barolo has high tannins and high acidity making it just as complex as your mooch kid. This rich red wine is said to have a taste that lingers, which probably sounds just like a certain child you know. Dealing with a grown-up child who moves out of your house only to move back in six months later has been proven to cause mild depression and an increase in alcohol consumption. So, next time you welcome back your adult-baby accompanied only by his total lack of ambition, welcome a few bottles of Barolo along with him. Cheers to never *ever* being empty nesters!

LAMBRUSCO
"PUT ON SOME CLOTHES" WINE

LAMBRUSCO *goes great with a steadfast refusal to wear seasonally appropriate clothing.*

When your child refuses to wear a jacket in thirty-two degree weather, know that Lambrusco is a must for you this evening. This sparkling red is light bodied, just like your seven-year-old who is demanding to wear a tank top outside in January. It's frustrating enough that the child denied the coat, but it's even more annoying when they also started begging you for your coat later because they're freezing . . . *like you said they'd be.* Data shows that parents who drink Lambrusco in the winter months have far less anxiety and tend to experience less eye-rolling than parents who don't. So stock up on Lambrusco and maybe just avoid leaving the house altogether this winter. Sunlight and socialization are overrated, anyway.

NEW ZEALAND
PINOT NOIR
4AM WINE

Choose NEW ZEALAND PINOT NOIR *when your child likes to wake you up in the creepiest way possible.*

If your child likes to wake up at four in the morning and quietly stand at your bedside staring at you like a stalker about to attack, then New Zealand Pinot Noir is the wine for you. Experts say that this fruity wine has a flashy taste that can sneak up on you, just like the little apparition who appears at your bedside at the *same time every night*. New Zealand Pinot Noir possesses soft strawberry and cherry aromas making it quite enjoyable, unlike being woken up by a three-foot person breathing mere inches from your sleeping face. While experts cannot keep your nightwalker from scaring the hell out of you at all hours of the night, be assured that a glass of New Zealand Pinot Noir can help you forget that terrifying episode . . . at least until tomorrow night.

RIOJA
CLAUSTROPHOBIC WINE

Pair **RIOJA** *with the child who won't let go of your leg.*

If your tot seems unable to walk without being attached to your thigh when out in public places, we are confident that Rioja will help restore some of your freedom. The crisp refreshing taste of this light red wine will have you feeling loose and free, whereas your toddler has you feeling trapped and claustrophobic. The constant weight of a small human constantly tugging on you can drive just about any mother insane, but experts say that two to three glasses of Rioja will have you revived and ready to face another day of entrapment in no time. It just depends on how fast you chug it.

SAVAGNIN NOIR
ORIFICE WINE

SAVAGNIN NOIR *goes great with foreign objects that have been stuck up a nose.*

When your reasonably intelligent child decides to lodge something small up his nasal cavity, we insist on drinking Savagnin Noir. This dark red wine is said to pair beautifully with vegetables, like that pea he just crammed into his nostril and accidentally inhaled. Data shows that this wine also compliments small, inedible objects, such as rocks, crayons, and game pieces. Sure, Savagnin Noir won't be able to help pay those aggravating emergency room bills, but don't worry—it looks like you won't be doling out Harvard tuition for Dylan at this rate anyway. So next time he sticks his miniature finger up there, maybe go ahead and let him. It's the safer and cheaper choice.

SANCERRE
THE LEGO WINE

Pair **SANCERRE** *with all things Lego.*

If your child has Excessive Dumping Disorder, then Sancerre is your wine of choice for this evening. Due to the dryness of this crisp white wine, it is reported to have an acidic burn that can make one's jaw tighten as you consume it, the exact reflex you have when you hear that damn Lego bin flip. There are very few acts of destruction that are more irritating than a freshly organized Lego bin being flipped by a miniature tyrant. Just the sound of every tiny colored piece crashing out onto the clean floor is enough to make you contemplate hurling your body out the nearest window. Tonight you can rest easy as you sip your glass(es) of Sancerre and not gives two shits about the piles of Legos scattered throughout the room. Until you step on one in the middle of the night. Cheers.

PINK MUSCATO
THE "WHY" WINE

PINK MUSCATO *wine pairs perfectly with being compared to Katie's mom.*

When your child constantly compares you to other mothers, take a seat and plunge into a bottle of Blush wine. This sweet rosé will do the trick when your child throws the very unoriginal "But Katie's mom lets *her* go to the movies with boys unsupervised! Why can't you be cool like Katie's mom?!" line at you. This type of wine is just about as easy to swallow as the fact that you are indeed *not* Katie's mother. What's even easier to swallow is the fact that you don't give a damn what Katie's mom does with her life. Wait, who the hell is Katie, again? Blush wines tend to be light and fresh, which will give you a break from all of the heavy tension. When your child throws all of your strict rules in your face as if they're an insult, go ahead and raise your glass and reply, "Are you complimenting my parenting choices, darling? Stop, you're making me *blush*." *Sip.*

SAUTERNES
MULTIPLE PERSONALITY WINE

SAUTERNES *pairs perfectly with a toddler's inconsistency.*

If your child loved chicken last week but now won't touch it with a ten-foot pole and has no interest in what was the *only* toy he liked last week, then Sauternes is the wine for you. This white wine has been described as heaven in a bottle, with strong fruity tones and hints of warm honey, making it the perfect pairing with tonight's dinner. Keeping up with a toddler's preferred food preferences is useless and draining, so take a break from the debating and prepare yourself a glass of Sauternes instead. Tonight, let's forgo the yelling and threatening of lives over three ounces of grilled poultry and which Disney character is best. He'll probably change his mind again tomorrow, or not . . . or maybe he will. I mean, who really knows. *Or cares.*

CORTESE
SCARED SHITLESS WINE

Choose **CORTESE** *when you get* THAT *phone call.*

If you answered the phone only to hear, "Mom, I'm fine, but . . . " then a bottle of Cortese will taste remarkable to you this evening. Cortese is a white wine that, when fermented correctly, exudes strong apple, peach, and honeydew flavors. Experts have revealed that honeydew is the perfect match for a serious lack of judgement, which sounds a lot like a certain teenager you know. After you recover from your acute heart attack, pop open a bottle of bubbly Cortese and plot your plan of action for the child whose main goal in life seems to be to repeatedly scaring the shit out of you. Data shows that Cortese has saved an astonishing amount of children from being eternally locked in their bedrooms. Drink Cortese and let the punk live to see another day.

SANGIOVESE
SMART ASS WINE

SANGIOVESE *goes great with adolescent smart-assery.*

When your preteen starts laying out attitude with some smart-ass comments in the mix, you've definitely earned a glass of Sangiovese tonight. Sangiovese is a tart rosé wine that has high tannins and high acidity. Some people find this wine sour and off-putting, just as you find your daughter to be when she refuses to wear anything you suggest. Whether it's a fight over the appropriate length of her shorts or crop tops that no twelve-year-old should be allowed to own, experts are sure that this wine is sure to do wonders for your sanity. Hide all the crop tops, bring out that wine, and try to forget how much your miniature smart ass reminds you of yourself.

ICE
I HATE CAILLOU WINE

Choose **ICE** *wine when children's television has you wanting to tear out your ovaries.*

When the annoying cries and whines of television's Caillou have you feeling emotionally wounded and never wanting to reproduce again, Ice wine should be your choice of beverage this evening. While Canada has many wonderful exports—maple syrup, Ryan Gosling, Tim Hortons coffee, and did we say Ryan Gosling?—neither Ice wine nor our bald-headed friend Caillou are among them, making this the pairing from hell. The sugars in this dessert wine are said to be extremely pungent making it hard to stand except in small sips, just like watching this shit show that for some reason is still being aired. Experts are looking into why Caillou continues to assault us with his obnoxious presence, but are confident that you will be able to withstand his torment only when consuming Ice wine.

CHAMPAGNE
EMPTY NEST WINE

Choose **CHAMPAGNE** *when your child finally moves out of your house.*

If you dropped your doe-eyed, barely legal teenager off in front of a college dormitory today, then we suggest only the finest sparkling wine for this ultimate celebration: Champagne. By some miracle, your child managed to obtain a diploma, is now furthering her education, and is out of your hair. Thank God. Now you can pray for her safety daily, obsessively stalk her Facebook page, and violently weep as you write painfully large checks for college tuition, all while poppin' bottles of Champagne. Champagne is a blend of Pinot and some other stuff . . . never mind the facts, statistics show that it tastes fantastic. You've been abused by this child for the last eighteen years, just drink up.

THE PERIODIC TABLE OF W(H)INE

Each pairing in this book has a corresponding sticker that you can add to your Periodic Table of W(h)ine chart that folds out here. Each time you try a new wine that we recommend, add your pairing sticker to the chart. The sticker grouping will reveal whether or not your kids have attitude problems, behavior problems, or just plain bad DNA!

Chardonnay

Vin Gris

Provence Rosé

Pinot Grigio

Sauternes

Sauvignon Blanc

Viognier

Prosecco

Sherry

Champagne

Pink Muscato

Verdejo

Muscat Blanc

Boxed Wine

Roussanne

Chenin Blanc

Ugni Blanc

Cortese

White Zinfandel

Riesling

Fiano

Sancerre

Grenache Blanc

Cava

Sangiovese

Rosado

Lambrusco

Pinot Noir Rosé

New Zealand Pinot Noir

Savagnin Noir

Pinot Noir

Lagrein

Syrah Rosé

Ice

Vinho Verde

White Merlot

Barolo

Cabernet Franc

Pinotage

Cotês du Rhône

Malbec

Merlot

Gamay

Bandol

Syrah

Freisa

Cabernet Sauvignon

Bourgogne

Barbera

Zinfandel

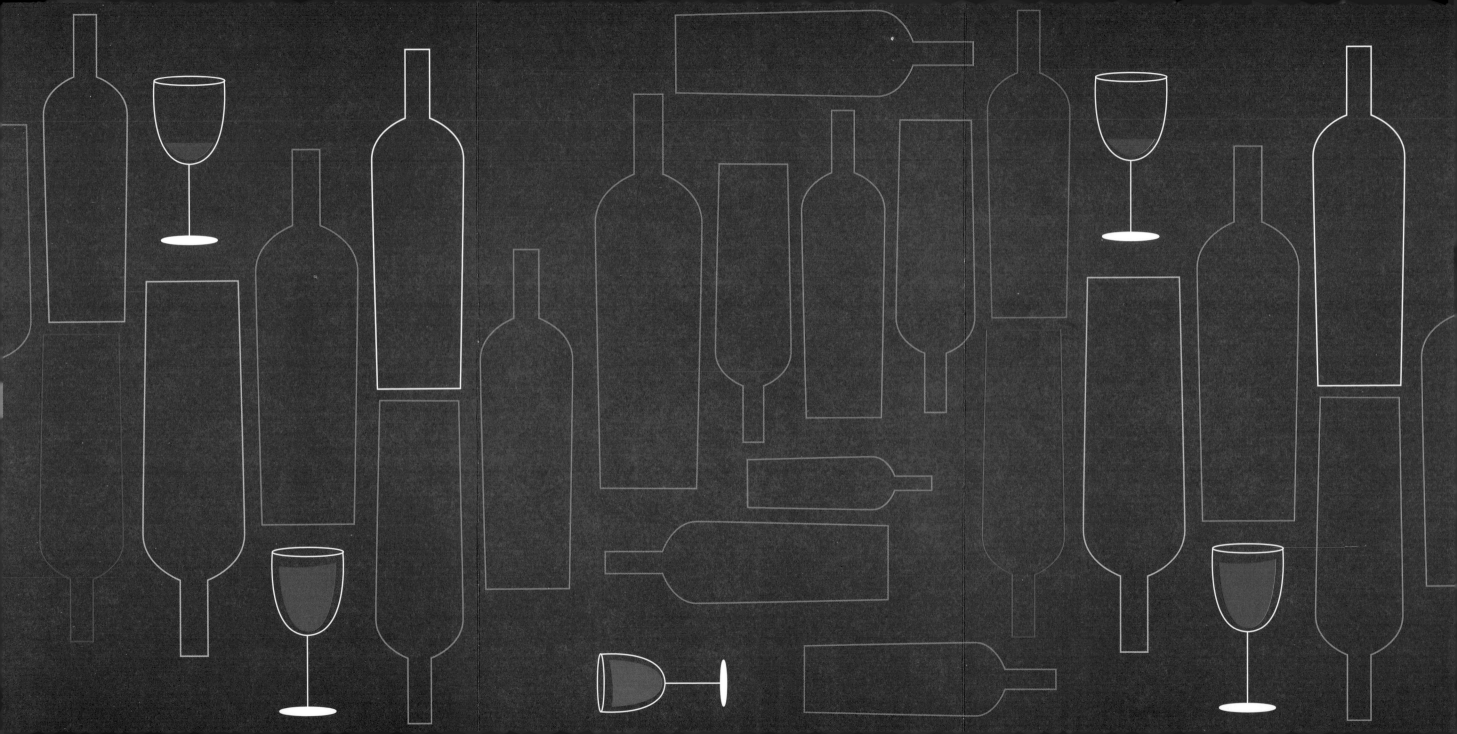

Weary Parent Wines

A Quick Look-Up Guide

ROTTEN ATTITUDE WINES

If you're suffering through some bad attitude from your kids today, here is a quick reference list for the wine for you. We know you don't have the strength to browse!

PINOTAGE

CHARDONNAY

RIOJA

Verdejo

PINOT GRIGIO

Provence Rose

PINK MUSCATO

Rosado

Sangiovese

Cabernet Franc

ZINFANDEL

SAUTERNES

Côtes du Rhône

If your problem today revolves around a specific crappy behavior, then we'd like to quickly direct you to these choices:

Viogner

MERLOT

Sauvignon Blanc

Muscat Blanc

MALBEC

Roussanne

Lambrusco

Pinot Noir Rosé

New Zealand Pinot Noir

any boxed wine

111

ROTTEN

DNA

WINES

Let's face it, sometimes the problem is just bad genes and there isn't a damn thing you can do about it. If that is the problem you're facing today, own it with one of these choice wine selections:

SAVAGNIN NOIR

Cortese

Gamay

Chenin Blanc

PINOT GRIGIO

SYRAH

Pinot Noir

UGNI BLANC

Bandol

LAGREIN

PROSECCO

Carménère

Tempranillo

Syrah Rosé

White Zinfandel

CHABLIS

PINOT GRIS   St. Laurent

Some days it's not even your kids that are driving you crazy, but your spouse. If you are finding it difficult not to strangle your significant other today, we recommend these wines guaranteed to help you keep your cool (and your vows):

ROTTEN LUCK WINES

Some days luck isn't on your side, and there isn't a single person to blame. Try any of these delectable beverages guaranteed to improve your luck and pluck:

Sherry

Riesling

FIANO

Sancerre

Grenache Blanc

Bourgogne

WHITE MERLOT

BAROLO

Cabernet Sauvignon

ICE

Freisa

Vinho Verde

BARBERA

CHAMPAGNE

PORT

CRÉMANT ROSÉ

Prosecco

CAVA

AMONTILLADO

Madeira

Is today a reason to celebrate? Perhaps you got to enjoy the bathroom uninterrupted? Or your child actually remembered where he last left his shoes?

Whatever the reason to celebrate, here's a quick list of wines meant for toasting:

ACKNOWLEDGMENTS

Let me start by giving all of the glory to God for allowing me to live out a newly found passion, as well as surrounding me with an amazing support system. I have been blessed beyond measure in my life. I grew up in a very strong family unit, have had irreplaceable friends throughout the years, and now I get to reach out to other moms and attempt to be their daily dose of laughter as they navigate one of the hardest jobs in the world. For that and endless of other reasons, I am thankful to Him. To my husband, who supports me in every aspect of life. I could walk into Mike's home office tomorrow and tell him that I wanted to build a business for designing glitter pinecone garlands, and he would be forming a business plan for it within the hour. He always has my back and pushes me to step outside my comfort zone and to never take "no" for an answer. Mike, I love you for being the risk-taker in this relationship. If it weren't for you, this book would not be in existence. I love you DIS MUCH. Forever and ever, babe. To my parents who have been dealing with my inability to commit to anything for longer than two years . . . I did it! I've stuck to this blog, and I'm not going anywhere! Thank you for raising me in a home where family comes first and anything is obtainable with hard work. Thank you to my mom for showing me what a strong woman looks like, and to my dad for always being my number-one fan. To my children (a.k.a. "child beasts") . . . I love you so much. Thank you for supplying me with an endless amount of writing material.

One day you will read this and get it, and I will be there for you to vent your frustrations. You are the reason I wake up in the morning (*entirely too early, since we're on the topic*) and the last thing I think about before I fall asleep. Berkley, you are my baby, my sweetheart. You came out of the womb independent, and that has never wavered. Your constant laughter and goofy personality bring a smile to anyone you come into contact with. Von, you are my extremely intelligent ball of energy, and the one who made me a Mommy. Your hardheadedness is a doozy for me currently, but I know that one day you'll be one strong man because of it.

Thank you to my editor, Jeannine! If you hadn't tracked me down via Facebook and multiple emails, this book would not be here today. For that, I am forever grateful to you. Thank you for taking a chance on me and guiding me through this journey to remember!

Last, but certainly not least, I would like to thank the fans of *Life as a Rambling Redhead*. The community I have built through this blog never ceases to amaze me. You women are funny, real, raw, brave, and not alone. I feel what you are feeling, I get what you are saying, and you are the reason I keep writing. Thank you so much for sharing what I have to say with others, for giving me feedback, for the endless messages that I can't always respond to (turns out keeping the child beasts alive is a full-time job), and— most of all— for your encouragement. You guys get me. You get my life, you get my sense of humor, you get why I call my darling children "beasts" and "child-terrorists." Thanks for joining me in this crazy journey called motherhood.

Oh, and thank you to my sophomore English teacher, Mr. Phillips, for telling me that I wasn't a good writer. You were truly my inspiration.

MEET THE REDHEAD

JENNIFER TODRYK is the sarcastic redhead behind the popular parenting blog *Life as a Rambling Redhead*. She started the blog with the expectation that only her family members would be reading along (if that . . .) and has loved watching it grow into something far bigger than she ever imagined. Jennifer resides in Dallas, Texas, where she raises her two child-beasts and is constantly picking up her husband's clothes off the floor in between diaper changes and butt wipings. She normally can be found at her local HomeGoods store, feeding her extreme addiction to home décor with a Starbucks latte in hand and two children strapped to a shopping cart. Jennifer loves being a mother more than anything but thinks that the occasional mandatory out-of-town business meeting sounds like a fabulous vacation.

Like *Life as a Rambling Redhead* on Facebook and follow along with the hilarity! Follow Jennifer on Instagram for awesome home-decorating inspiration @theramblingredhead.